Photos

by Alison Hawes

illustrated by Christiane Engel

T0372659

CAMBRIDGE
UNIVERSITY PRESS

UCL
Institute of Education

Here is my Dad.

Here is my Mum.

Here is my Grandma.

Here is my Grandpa.

Here is my sister.

Here is my brother.

And here is my bird!

Photos 🐦 Alison Hawes

Teaching notes written by Sue Bodman and Glen Franklin

Using this book

Developing reading comprehension

This simple story features a series of accidental photos as the parrot gets in the way of all attempts to compose a good photograph. A repetitive sentence structure is used to tell the story. The addition of 'And' on the final page creates a subtle challenge to self-monitoring one-to-one correspondence.

Grammar and sentence structure

- Text is well-spaced to support the development of one-to-one correspondence.
- One line of text and highly predictable changes in the noun supported by clear illustrations.
- In contexts where children are learning English as an additional language, support by rehearsing the sentence structure orally before introducing the book.

Word meaning and spelling

- Use letter information to check use of familiar use of vocabulary ('Grandpa', 'Grandma').
- Reinforce recognition of frequently occurring words ('Here', 'is', 'my').

Curriculum links

Literacy – Plan a menu for the barbecue in the garden, presenting the items in a list. Children could then illustrate the list. This activity could be done as a class, in small groups or as an individual task.

Language development – Ask the children to retell the story using the same sentence structure ('Here is my …') with members of their own family and substituting a different animal that keeps getting in the camera shot.

Learning Outcomes

Children can:

- understand that print carries meaning and is read from left to right
- develop awareness of capital letter forms
- track one line of simple repetitive text.

A guided reading lesson

Book Introduction

Give a book to each child and read the title. Ask the children to point to the title and read it.

Orientation

Give a brief orientation to the text: *The girl in this book is trying to take photos of her family. But her pet bird keeps getting in the way.*

Preparation

Page 2: Say: *The girl says 'Here is my dad.'* Read the text slowly enough for the children to point to each word carefully in their copy as you read. Repeat and support if necessary. Say: *Well done. Make sure you point carefully when you read by yourself.*

Page 4: Draw attention to the change in person on each page by asking the child to check the picture and locate the word that looks right. *Who is she taking a photo of now? You think it could be mum? Read through the sentence and find the word 'mum'. That's right. I can hear /m/. That words looks right. Does it make sense with the picture? Yes, it does.*

Turn through pages 6 to 13, making sure that the naming vocabulary is familiar to the children. Make links between